California Ranchos

by Natalie M. Rosinsky

Content Adviser: Nancy Lemke,
Author and Historian,
Bonita, California

Reading Adviser: Susan Kesselring, M.A.,
Literacy Educator,
Rosemount–Apple Valley–Eagan (Minnesota) School District

COMPASS POINT BOOKS
MINNEAPOLIS, MINNESOTA

Compass Point Books
3109 West 50th Street, #115
Minneapolis, MN 55410

Visit Compass Point Books on the Internet at *www.compasspointbooks.com*
or e-mail your request to *custserv@compasspointbooks.com*

On the cover: *The California Ranchos* by Joseph Holbrook.

Photographs ©: Courtesy of the artist, Joseph Holbrook, cover, 15; Prints Old and Rare, back cover (far left); Library of Congress, back cover, 20, 32; Corbis, 4; Courtesy of the Bancroft Library, University of California, Berkeley, 5, 17; San Diego Historical Society, 7, 33; The Granger Collection, New York, 8, 10, 31, 37; Laguna Art Museum, Gift of Nancy Dustin Wall Moure, 9; From the collection of the Mission Inn Foundation and Museum, Riverside, Calif., 11; Courtesy Rancho Los Alamitos, 12; Marilyn "Angel" Wynn, 14; California Historical Society, Harry Humphrey Moore, *Woman Playing Guitar*, TN-2920, 16; Courtesy of Rancho Los Cerritos Historic Site, Eliza Bone, 18; North Wind Picture Archives, 19, 23, 24; Los Altos History Museum, Los Altos, Calif., 21; Christie's Images/Corbis, 22; The Huntington Library, 25; Smithsonian American Art Museum, Washington, D.C./Art Resource, N.Y., 26; Crocker Art Museum, E. B. Crocker Collection, 28; California Historical Society, James Walker, *Roping the Bear*, Santa Margarita Rancho of Juan Forester, TN-4043, 29; The Society of California Pioneers, 34; Photograph Provided Courtesy of the Command Museum, MCRDSD/Colonel Charles Waterhouse artist, 35; MPI/Getty Images, 36; Doheny Memorial Library, University of Southern California, 39; Charles Mann/Corbis, 40; John Elk III, 41.

Managing Editor: Catherine Neitge
Page Production: Bobbie Nuytten
Photo Researcher: Marcie C. Spence
Cartographer: XNR Productions, Inc.
Library Consultant: Kathleen Baxter

Creative Director: Keith Griffin
Editorial Director: Carol Jones

Library of Congress Cataloging-in-Publication Data
Rosinsky, Natalie M. (Natalie Myra)
 California ranchos / by Natalie Rosinsky.
   p. cm.—(We the people)
 Includes bibliographical references and index.
 ISBN-13: 978-0-7565-1633-8 (hardcover)
 ISBN-10: 0-7565-1633-1 (hardcover)
 ISBN-13: 978-0-7565-1808-0 (paperback)
 ISBN-10: 0-7565-1808-3 (paperback)
 1. California—History—To 1846—Juvenile literature. 2. Ranch life—California—History—19th century—Juvenile literature. 3. Ranches—California—History—19th century—Juvenile literature. 4. Spanish Americans—California—History—19th century—Juvenile literature. 5. Mexican Americans—California—History—19th century—Juvenile literature.
I. Title. II. We the people (Series) (Compass Point Books)
 F864.R78 2006
 979.4'03—dc22   2005025085

TABLE OF CONTENTS

"GENTLEMEN" AT WAR

The adobe walls of the presidio glowed in the sunshine of November 1836. This fort in the seaside city of Monterey was the largest in California, a territory that then belonged to Mexico. Spanish-speaking government officials who lived in this capital city had frequent business at the presidio. Wealthy rancheros, who owned large nearby

Monterey was the capital of California when it was ruled by Mexico.

estates called ranchos, often visited there or stopped at the residence of Governor Nicolas Gutierrez. Because these rancheros owned huge cattle herds, traded many items, and held power over other people on their ranchos, they worked closely with local government officials. But this day would be different.

Typical dress of elite Californios

The wealthiest ranchero families led elegant lives. One American visitor described these Californios, as they called themselves, as "gentlemen of the first class both in manners and habits." Yet some

5

of the wealthy Californios were not happy being governed by Mexico.

On that November day, they came to the presidio, and 27-year-old Juan Bautista Alvarado led them in a revolt against Mexico. It was an easy victory for the rebels, who had planned ahead by sending a gift of whiskey to the presidio. They knew that drunken soldiers would not fight well! Only one cannon shot was fired at the home of the governor, and he surrendered. From December 1836 to July 1837, Alvarado was the revolutionary governor of California. Although Mexico won back control of the territory, Alvarado and his ranchero supporters stayed in power until 1842.

Such easy victories and exchanges of power were the exception in California. They came after a long, bloody history of exploration and colonization. Its costs were highest for people whose background or race separated them from wealthy "gentlemen" such as Juan Bautista Alvarado.

TRAINING THE NATIVES

Spanish exploration led to the rancho way of life in California. Juan Rodriguez Cabrillo explored the area in the 16th century, yet Spain did not begin active settlement of California for two more centuries.

Juan Rodriguez Cabrillo

In 1769, Gaspar de Portolá led an expedition from Mexico to what is now San Diego. Soldiers and two Catholic priests, Fathers Junípero Serra and Juan Crespi, accompanied him. Father Crespi described how many of the native people met them with bows held loose, "which is a sign of peace," and how they "brought us an abundant present of [food]." In time, this hospitality backfired on the California

Father Serra traveled with Gaspar de Portolá's expedition to California.

natives. When more Spaniards arrived, they brought permanent, harmful changes to the natives' way of life.

Father Serra and his fellow priests believed it was best for the natives to learn to live like Spaniards and be converted to Christianity. Once converted and trained, the natives could help occupy more land for Spain. Over the next 50 years, the priests established 21 missions throughout California for these purposes.

The Spaniards, though, did not respect the customs of the many different tribes in California. Father Geronimo Boscana wrote that a typical California native had eyes that "are never uplifted, but like those of the swine, are cast to the earth. Truth is not in him." While a few priests won the natives' trust, most priests felt that they had the right to use any methods needed to convert and train natives.

These new converts, whom the Spaniards called neophytes, were forced to live and work at the missions. They farmed, constructed buildings, made tools and other items, cooked, and tended cattle. To feed the Spaniards and

An 1832 oil painting of San Gabriel was the first ever oil of a California mission.

Soldiers at the presidio captured natives who tried to escape.

natives, huge ranches with livestock and food crops developed around the missions.

Neophytes learned many skills, but they could be punished if they disobeyed. Soldiers at nearby presidios helped the priests keep order at the missions. Sometimes, the soldiers tracked and caught natives who tried to escape. Because of the heavy workload and brutal treatment, some neophytes died. Many more died from diseases that the Spanish unknowingly carried to California. By 1823, when the last mission was built, the native population of more than 150,000 people had been reduced to fewer than 30,000.

LAND FOR THE ASKING

Much of the land along the California coast was used by missions for their herds and crops. Missionaries said that this land would someday be given back to neophytes who had learned Spanish ways. Meanwhile, Spanish soldiers became interested in other California land.

When they left the army, some soldiers lived in villages called pueblos with their families. Former soldiers who married native women had families whose mixed

The land surrounding the missions was used for herds, orchards, and crops.

11

background was called mestizo. To support their families, some of these men asked the Spanish government for California land of their own. In 1784, a few received grants of land. These became the first ranchos.

Local governors and presidio commanders had the legal right to give land away. Individuals would describe the particular piece of land they wanted in writing. In 1801, one former soldier wrote, "The distance I ask is from the banks of the Santa Ana River … more than a league

Rancho Los Alamitos (Ranch of the Little Cottonwoods) in Long Beach began as a simple adobe building in the early 1800s.

12

(about 2.6 miles or 4 kilometers). [F]rom the highway to the house will be about a league and a half; from there to the mountains about three leagues; and toward the south I ask as far as Ranas … about a league and a half." Since a square league, or legua, is about 4,400 acres (1,760 hectares) even the smaller ranchos were quite large.

Along with this written description, the future landowner submitted a hand-drawn map, called a *diseño*, showing landmarks such as rivers, hills, any odd-shaped trees, and even any large animal skeletons. He also had to promise to build a house, grow crops, and raise livestock there.

About 30 ranchos were granted before 1821, when Mexico won its independence from Spain. The rancho way of life then became widespread. Between 1821 and 1846, the newly established Mexican government granted more than 700 new ranchos in California. The largest of these were owned by members of a few, related families with aristocratic backgrounds. In Spain, many of these families had already been landowners. New wealthy rancheros,

13

Most native people did not receive the mission lands they were promised.

including Juan Bautista Alvarado, influenced laws and political decisions in California.

In 1834, Governor Jose Figueroa announced that mission land no longer belonged to the church. Half of all mission land was now supposed to be returned to native neophytes, but this did not happen. Many received no land. Other natives were cheated by what they did get. A former neophyte from Mission Santa Cruz said that his people received only "old mares that were no longer productive and very old rams." Without other tools or supplies, the mission land his people now owned "did not do the Indians any good." Since most neophytes could not read and were not familiar with the legal system, they had little chance of getting land or goods owed them.

The richest of the new California rancheros were a different class of people from the soldiers who acquired the

A rancho's main house was often built of adobe bricks.

smaller plots of land. These wealthy rancheros often came from proud, wealthy families that for generations had already owned land in Spain or Mexico. They would not marry native women, as some soldiers had, and have mestizo children.

Aristocratic women were addressed by the title "doña."

In California between 1821 and 1846, the rancho way of life further separated people by race and skin color. Since these aristocratic rancheros often asked for and received more than 11 square leagues of land, their vast holdings and great wealth also set them apart. The richest rancheros and their wives were addressed by the respectful titles "don" and "doña." In Spanish, these words mean "nobleman" and "lady."

WORKERS AND SERVANTS

While a large rancho owner proudly rode across his land, planning projects and supervising laborers, the actual hard work was done by natives or mestizos. These poorer people also did the indoor chores, supervised by the doña. As one priest described both mission and rancho life, "If there is anything to be done, the Indian has to do it; if he fails to do it, nothing will be done."

More than 4,000 former neophytes moved onto ranchos, where they worked for food and shelter but received little or no pay. They were like serfs who once labored for European lords and ladies. Because their native ways of life and communities were gone, neophytes had

Wealthy rancheros supervised the work performed by laborers.

17

few choices other than to work on ranchos.

Most ranchos were built in a similar way. The main family house had adobe walls and a log roof covered with more adobe, dirt, or tiles. This large house was usually one story tall, but a few grand rancho houses had two stories. In the Spanish fashion, this main house was often built around an open courtyard, where family members could gather with visitors. Often, living quarters for household servants were attached to the main house. Most other

18

The large Rancho Los Cerritos in Long Beach was built in 1844.

workers lived in smaller buildings on the rancho property. Some workers lived in pueblos, which might be located on rancho land or just outside it.

Many ranchos had between 11 and 32 workers, but the largest ranchos had up to 100 workers. Francisca Carrillo Vallejo, the wife of General Mariano Guadalupe Vallejo, one of the wealthiest rancheros, claimed that in her large family of 16 children (a typical size family in those days), each one "has a servant who has no other duty than to care for him or her. I have two servants for myself." Wealthy doñas and their children performed some chores necessary to the running of the rancho, but their tasks were light compared to the labor of native and mestizo workers.

Francisca Carrillo Vallejo

19

Besides living quarters, a large rancho's buildings included a stable and workshops for tasks such as carpentry. Some ranchos also had their own small church or chapel. Because ranchos were isolated from each other, they became little towns of their own.

On these ranchos, girls and women sewed, cooked, cleaned, washed and ironed clothing, and tended the gardens and fruit orchards surrounding the main house. Boys and men made shoes, leather and metal farm equipment, and furniture. They farmed wheat, corn, and bean fields. Men tended sheep and the larger cattle herds that were a necessary part of rancho life.

Smaller ranchos were run somewhat differently. Juana

An 1850 illustration of mestizo women carrying water and washing clothes

Briones owned and maintained several small ranchos in and near what is today San Francisco. The wife of a former soldier, this hardworking mestizo woman became well-known for her skills and kindness as a healer. Briones drew upon native peoples' knowledge of healing herbs. With just a few servants, she and her many children cared for their land and animals. She also helped

Juana Briones

women give birth, and tended sick or injured people from all backgrounds. She often refused payment for her help, saying "If they get well, I am satisfied." After her husband became a dangerous drunkard, she sought and got a divorce from him. For many years after that, Briones continued her ranching and healing work.

21

COWBOYS AND "CALIFORNIA BANKNOTES"

The first cowboys in North America were the native and mestizo ranch hands called *vaqueros*. This name came from the Spanish word *vaca*, which means cow.

A vaquero painted by noted artist Frederic Remington

Vaqueros were experts in using their lariats, or braided ropes, to herd and round up cattle. Large hats called sombreros kept the sun off their heads. Leather trousers, later called chaps, protected their legs from rough chaparral bushes. Sharp, shiny spurs jingled on their boots and prodded their sluggish horses.

Despite the frequent injuries that vaqueros suffered

22

doing their jobs, their sons looked forward to joining them at work. The boys played at roping fence posts as soon as they could hold a small lariat in their hands. By the age of 6 or 7, these boys were happily roping moving targets such as rabbits or chickens.

A vaquero and his horse gallop to lasso a steer.

Roping was a vital skill during the springtime roundup of cattle for branding. Each large rancho had its own brands, or special marks, burned into the hides of cattle to identify their owner. In late summer or early autumn, another kind of roundup called a *matanza* was held. Its purpose was to gather together animals for slaughter. Vaqueros usually separated between 50 and 100 of the fattest, full-grown steers from the large herds that sometimes

23

Rancheros and vaqueros branded longhorn cattle in the spring.

covered nearly a half mile of land. Thick clouds of dust, loud roars from angry and frightened animals, and shouts from busy vaqueros filled the air during this exciting, dangerous event.

Matanzas were held to slaughter animals for trade rather than food. Although beef was frequently eaten on ranchos, fat and hides were important trade items. Some

24

rancho workers had the hot, smelly job of boiling beef fat down into liquid tallow, used to make soap and candles. Noisy wooden carts carried leather sacks filled with tallow to seaside ports.

Rancheros traded the tallow with ships' captains from the eastern United States, England, and other countries. In exchange, they received manufactured and fancy items such as guns, fine furniture, clothing, and books. Cowhides used for shoes or leather were also traded. Hides were traded so often that they became known as "California banknotes."

Indian workers boiled beef fat to make tallow.

CELEBRATIONS AND COMPETITIONS

Rancho life held fun as well as work. One visitor remarked about the "powerful impression of cheerfulness and gaiety" he experienced as a rancho guest. The Catholic religion was the reason for many celebrations. At Christmastime, the entire rancho household observed the Spanish tradition of Las Posadas. Over several nights, they acted out the

Mission churches were the center of religious and social life.

search of Mary and Joseph for a place to stay for the birth of the baby Jesus. Boys and girls also celebrated the feast day of the saint for which they were named. Birthdays and anniversaries provided other reasons for celebration. Because ranchos were often so far apart, hospitality toward guests was an important tradition in all ranchero families.

Weddings were celebrated with weeklong parties. A guest at one rancho wedding in 1838 wrote about "dancing being kept up all the night" and about the "picnics in the woods" held in the afternoons. He joked that by week's end, "I had been so exhausted … that I was glad to escape [the party]." During such occasions, children especially enjoyed one rancho tradition involving eggshells hollowed out by family members and servants. The children carefully filled the shells with perfume or confetti and then tossed the shells so they broke open for a wonderful surprise.

Fast dances called fandangos were part of such celebrations, where everyone wore their fanciest clothing. People also sang, listened to music, and enjoyed eating

27

meat and corn dishes flavored with hot chile peppers. Spicy foods were so popular that it was a compliment to say a meal "was capable of raising the dead!"

At some gatherings, rancho owners and vaqueros displayed their riding and roping skills. The single men hoped to impress their sweethearts enough to get them to marry them. Horse races were common. During what

California artist Charles Christian Nahl painted The Fandango, *a romantic view of the rancheros, in 1878.*

Rancheros captured bears for animal fights.

came to be called rodeos, vaqueros competed against one another as they roped running bulls. Sometimes, riders showed off by racing along on horseback, bending down to pick up small objects from the ground.

At such gatherings, people sometimes bet on fights between roosters or between a bull and a bear. The nephew of ranchero Mariano Vallejo described the bloody conclusion of one animal fight, when the bear "got his claw into the bull's mouth, pulled the tongue out still further, and then bit it off." Hunting for bears or deer was another rancho social event.

A visitor to several large ranchos observed that workers as well as the family took part in celebrations. His remarks fit the view of Doña Vallejo, who said "[W]e act as good parents to our servants. … [W]e treat our servants rather as friends than as servants." Yet her daughters dressed in fine imported clothes made of satin and lace, while servants wore coarser skirts and serapes. The sons of wealthy rancheros were taught to read and write, while most servants were not. The actual sons and daughters of an aristocratic ranchero did not labor the way native and mestizo servants did.

A TIME OF REVOLT

Because California was far away from the capital of Mexico, some so-called Californios believed they could govern themselves better than Mexico did. This led to the brief revolt that Juan Bautista Alvarado led in 1836.

At the same time that Californios were feeling distant from Mexico, the United States was growing closer. Rancheros in particular had mixed feelings about these new connections.

Some rancheros welcomed educated American traders into their families. After learning Spanish and converting to Catholicism, Americans Alfred Robinson and Abel Stearns married the daughters of wealthy rancheros.

Juan Bautista Alvarado

31

Jedediah Smith's party crossed the burning Mojave Desert to get to California.

They became respected members of rancho society. Not all American newcomers, however, cared to fit in to the rancho way of life. In 1826, Jedediah Smith had led the first American fur trappers across the Rocky Mountains and into California. Rough trappers and land-hungry settlers continued to journey to California throughout the 1840s.

Pío Pico, the last Mexican governor of California, worried about the number of Americans settling in California to farm and conduct business. He asked, "What are we to do … ? [S]trangers are overrunning our fertile plains, and gradually outnumbering us ... Shall these incursions go on unchecked, until we shall become strangers in our own land?" Pico thought that California would be better off if it became part of France or England.

Pío Pico

A few rancheros, however, such as General Mariano Vallejo, welcomed the idea of California becoming part of the United States. Vallejo did not have the chance to pursue his goal peacefully, however. On June 14, 1846, in the town of Sonoma, California, about 30 American settlers, trappers, and explorers forced their way into this leader's home. These rough, armed men—many

33

The historic bear flag, which was photographed in 1890,
was destroyed in the 1906 San Francisco earthquake.

barefoot and wearing coyote and wolf skins—were deter-
mined that California become a country in its own right.
They abducted Vallejo. In the town square, they raised
a flag of their own design. Decorated with a roughly
drawn star and bear, it had the words CALIFORNIA
REPUBLIC handwritten across its middle.

This incident became known as the Bear Flag
Revolt. It did not result in California's independence, but
it did soon encourage further outbreaks of violence led by

American explorer John Charles Frémont. Disagreements continued to grow between the United States and Mexico over Mexican territory, including Texas. In July 1846, a war officially began between the two countries. When the United States won the Mexican War in 1848 and signed the Treaty of Guadalupe Hidalgo, Mexico lost most of its northern land. California came under American rule.

The Americans lost the Battle of San Pasqual in California but won the Mexican War.

"THESE BE YOUR BEST GOLD FIELDS"

The Treaty of Guadalupe Hidalgo said that the rancheros could keep whatever land they could show they owned legally. Yet these landowners soon found their holdings under attack. In January 1848, gold was discovered at Sutter's Mill near Coloma in northern California. Thousands of eager miners rushed to California in 1849,

Thousands of fortune hunters rushed to California to search for gold.

hoping to make their fortunes. These so-called 49ers did not care if they trespassed on rancho land. They cut down trees, dammed up creeks, and tore up land while seeking gold. Elderly ranchero Luis Peralta thought differently about where the gold really lay. He told his family to continue to "Plant your lands, and reap; these be your best gold fields, for all must eat while they live."

Some Americans traveled to California because they wanted to own and farm their own land. However, like the gold-seekers, these new settlers did not care that rancheros held grants to thousands of acres. They settled or squatted on rancho land that they claimed for themselves. After California became a state

Wagon trains of settlers headed west to California.

in 1850, its new government passed a law to settle such conflicting claims. But the Land Grant Act of 1851 did not help many rancheros.

Some Spanish and Mexican land grants were set aside, while others were maintained. But some rancheros had to

Land grants on territory formerly owned by Mexico came under attack.

spend years and enormous sums of money to win their cases in court. Juana Briones was one rancho owner who fought for 10 years and took her case all the way to the Supreme Court. She won and was able to keep her land.

Vicente Lugo, a prominent Californio, lost his rancho after California became a state.

In other instances, though, the years and money that rancheros spent to win their court cases brought defeat alongside victory. These rancheros had to sell off much of their property in order to pay lawyers and other fees.

Vicente Lugo lost most of his 30,000-acre (12,000-hectare) estate this way and remarked that he "sacrificed even the house in which [his family] lived." By the 1890s, the era of many great ranchos was over.

RANCHOS TODAY

Today, Mexican-Americans in California continue to honor traditions from their past. Many observe the Roman Catholic religion that was so important to rancheros. The food, music, and dance that were part of rancho life continue as well. These customs, along with rodeos, have also spread to other parts of the country.

Our understanding of the rich and complex history of the ranchos continues to grow. In 1997, Juana Briones became the first woman to be honored with a San Francisco landmark plaque. A school and park have also been

Rodeos, which began in the rancho days,
remain popular today.

named in her honor.

Yet most of the adobe buildings that marked the ranchos are gone. A few, like the Boronda Adobe in Monterey County, have been saved and restored by historians. Groups of interested citizens are working to save the remains of Briones' home in Palo Alto as a historical monument.

The Royal Presidio Chapel is all that remains of the Monterey Presidio founded in 1770.

Most rancho buildings, though, have been destroyed over time. Today, cities such as San Jose, Salinas, San Diego, and Los Angeles flourish on what was once rancho land. It remains up to students of history to remember the ranchos.

GLOSSARY

abducted—taken away by force

adobe—sun-dried clay bricks used in buildings

colonization—the settlement of territory by people from another country and the control by that country

confetti—small pieces of colorful paper tossed into the air during celebrations

convert—to change from one religion or faith to another

gaiety—happy or joyful feelings

landmarks—objects that help identify a location

presidio—a fort for Mexican or Spanish soldiers

serapes—wool cloth worn as shawls around people's shoulders and upper arms

serfs—people who labored without pay on a particular piece of land and who could be sold along with the land

DID YOU KNOW?

- Ranchos also existed in other Southwestern areas conquered by Spain and later ruled by Mexico. After the Mexican War, these territories became the states of Arizona, New Mexico, and Texas.

- The value of a cowhide called a California banknote ranged between $1 and $3. In today's currency, the value would be between $23 and $70.

- The old-fashioned English word for cowboy—*buckaroo*—comes from people mispronouncing the Spanish word *vaquero*. Not until the 1860s did the word *cowboy* become a popular term.

- In the early 19th century, vaqueros were invited to Hawaii to help people there learn how to manage cattle.

- Richard Henry Dana's classic tale about life at sea aboard a trading ship, titled *Two Years Before the Mast*, also details what he saw of rancho life and the hide trade.

- The bear flag flown during the so-called Bear Flag Revolt was designed and made by William Todd, a nephew of Abraham Lincoln. California adopted a bear flag as its state flag in 1911.

IMPORTANT DATES

Timeline

1542	Juan Rodriguez Cabrillo explores the south and central California coast
1769	Gaspar de Portolá explores as far north as present-day San Francisco; Father Junípero Serra founds the first of 21 missions
1784	First land grants awarded to former soldiers
1821	Mexico gains independence from Spain
1834	Mission land becomes available for ranchos
1836	Juan Bautista Alvarado declares California a free state, independent of Mexico
1846	Bear Flag Revolt occurs; Mexican War begins
1848	United States wins Mexican War and the Treaty of Guadalupe Hidalgo is signed; gold is discovered
1850	California becomes a state
1851	Land Grant Act passes and rancho land claims are reviewed
1890	Many large ranchos no longer exist

Important People

Juan Bautista Alvarado (1809–1882)
Ranchero who led unsuccessful 1836 revolt to make California independent of Mexico

Jose Figueroa (1782–1835)
Mexican governor of California who in 1834 legally removed mission land from church ownership

John Charles Frémont (1813–1890)
American explorer who joined in the Bear Flag Revolt and later served as a senator from the state of California

Pío Pico (1801–1894)
Last Mexican governor of California who granted many ranchos

Father Junípero Serra (1713–1784)
Franciscan priest who arrived in California in 1769 with Gaspar de Portolá (1723–1784) and established the first missions

Mariano Guadalupe Vallejo (1808–1890)
Wealthy ranchero who favored California becoming part of the United States; he was abducted during the Bear Flag Revolt

WANT TO KNOW MORE?

At the Library

Freedman, Russell. *In the Days of the Vaqueros: America's First True Cowboys*.
New York: Clarion, 2001.

Garland, Sherry. *Valley of the Moon: The Diary of Maria Rosalia de Milagros*.
New York: Scholastic, 2001.

La Pierre, Yvette. *Welcome to Josephina's World, 1824: Growing Up on
America's Southwest Frontier*. Middleton, Wis.: Pleasant Company, 1999.

Richter, Glenda. *The Stories of Juana Briones, Alta California Pioneer*. Bonita,
Calif.: Bookhandler Press, 2002.

On the Web

For more information on the *California Ranchos*, use FactHound
to track down Web sites related to this book.

1. Go to *www.facthound.com*

2. Type in a search word related to this book
   or this book ID: 0756516331

3. Click on the *Fetch It* button.

Your trusty FactHound will fetch the best Web sites for you!

On the Road

Boronda Adobe Casa
333 Boronda Road
Salinas, CA 93902
831/757-8085
Restoration of a 19th-century
rancho

The Bowers Museum
2002 N. Main St.
Santa Clara, CA 92706
714/567-3600
Permanent exhibit about life at
the missions and ranchos

Look for more We the People books about this era:

The Alamo
ISBN 0-7565-0097-4

The Arapaho and Their History
ISBN 0-7565-0831-2

The Battle of the Little Bighorn
ISBN 0-7565-0150-4

The Buffalo Soldiers
ISBN 0-7565-0833-9

The California Gold Rush
ISBN 0-7565-0041-9

The Cherokee and Their History
ISBN 0-7565-1273-5

The Chumash and Their History
ISBN 0-7565-0835-5

The Creek and Their History
ISBN 0-7565-0836-3

The Erie Canal
ISBN 0-7565-0679-4

Great Women of Pioneer America
ISBN 0-7565-1269-7

Great Women of the Old West
ISBN 0-7565-0099-0

The Iroquois and Their History
ISBN 0-7565-1272-7

The Klondike Gold Rush
ISBN 0-7565-1630-7

The Lewis and Clark Expedition
ISBN 0-7565-0044-3

The Library of Congress
ISBN 0-7565-1631-5

The Louisiana Purchase
ISBN 0-7565-0210-1

The Mexican War
ISBN 0-7565-0841-X

The Ojibwe and Their History
ISBN 0-7565-0843-6

The Oregon Trail
ISBN 0-7565-0045-1

The Pony Express
ISBN 0-7565-0301-9

The Powhatan and Their History
ISBN 0-7565-0844-4

The Pueblo and Their History
ISBN 0-7565-1274-3

The Santa Fe Trail
ISBN 0-7565-0047-8

The Sioux and Their History
ISBN 0-7565-1275-1

The Trail of Tears
ISBN 0-7565-0101-6

The Transcontinental Railroad
ISBN 0-7565-0153-9

The Wampanoag and Their History
ISBN 0-7565-0847-9

The War of 1812
ISBN 0-7565-0848-7

The Wilderness Road
ISBN 0-7565-1637-4

A complete list of We the People titles is available on our Web site:
www.compasspointbooks.com

47

INDEX

About the Author

Natalie M. Rosinsky is the award-winning author of more than 90 publications, including 10 books about Native American tribes. She writes about science, history, economics, social studies, and popular culture. One of her two cats usually sits near her computer as she works in Mankato, Minnesota. Natalie earned graduate degrees from the University of Wisconsin and has been a high school teacher and college professor as well as a corporate trainer.